Junior Great Books

SAMPLER

JUNIOR GREAT BOOKS®

SAMPLER

The Great Books Foundation
A nonprofit educational organization

Junior Great Books® is a registered trademark of the Great Books Foundation.

Shared Inquiry™ is a trademark of the Great Books Foundation.

The contents of this publication include proprietary trademarks and copyrighted materials and may be used or quoted only with permission and appropriate credit to the Foundation.

Copyright © 2011 by The Great Books Foundation
Chicago, Illinois
All rights reserved
ISBN 978-1-933147-77-2

First Printing
2 4 6 8 9 7 5 3 1
Printed in the United States of America

Published and distributed by

THE GREAT BOOKS FOUNDATION
A nonprofit educational organization

35 East Wacker Drive, Suite 400

Chicago, IL 60601

www.greatbooks.org

Contents

1   INTRODUCTION
    6   Dos and Don'ts in Discussion
    8   Shared Inquiry Discussion Guidelines

11 OOKA AND THE HONEST THIEF
    *Japanese folktale
    as told by I. G. Edmonds*

21 LETTING SWIFT RIVER GO
    Jane Yolen

39 THE EMPEROR'S NEW CLOTHES
    Hans Christian Andersen

55 GLOSSARY

INTRODUCTION

Welcome to Junior Great Books! In this program, you will be reading stories and discussing your ideas about them. Before you begin, here are some important things to know.

The stories in Junior Great Books will make you wonder about things. You might wonder what a word means or why a character does something.

Your teacher will read the story to you and ask you to think of questions you have about it. Any question you have about the story is worth asking.

The teacher will write down all questions so everyone can help think about them.

Some questions you can answer right away. You will talk or write about other questions later on.

You will get to read the story again and do activities that help you think more about it. Your teacher will also ask questions about parts of the story.

When it is time for the discussion, you will sit in a circle or square so you can see and hear one another.

Your teacher will start the discussion by asking a question about what the story means. This question will have more than one good answer. The teacher will ask all of you to say more about your ideas.

Your teacher isn't trying to get you to say the "right" answer to the discussion question. It is all right if people disagree about the best answer. At the end of the discussion everyone will understand the story better, even if you have different ideas about it. This kind of discussion is called a Shared Inquiry™ discussion.

Dos and Don'ts in Discussion

DO
Let other people talk, and listen to what they say.

DON'T
Talk while other people are talking.

DO
Share your ideas about the story. You may have an idea no one else has thought of.

DON'T
Be afraid to say what you're thinking about the story.

DO
Be polite when you disagree with someone.

DON'T
Get angry when someone disagrees with you.

DO
Pay attention to the person who is talking.

DON'T
Do things that make it hard for people to pay attention.

Shared Inquiry Discussion Guidelines

Following these guidelines in Shared Inquiry discussion will help everyone share ideas about the story and learn from one another.

1. Listen to or read the story twice before the discussion.

2. Discuss only the story that everyone has read.

3 Support your ideas with evidence from the story.

4 Listen to other people's ideas. You may agree or disagree with someone's answer, or ask a question about it.

5 Expect the teacher to only ask questions.

"This is too much," Gonta protested.

Ooka and the Honest Thief

*Japanese folktale
as told by I. G. Edmonds*

One day, Yahichi, owner of a rice store, came to Ooka's court, complaining that each night some of his rice disappeared.

"It is such a small amount that I hesitate to trouble your Honorable Honor," Yahichi said, touching the ground with his head to show proper respect for the great magistrate. "But I am reminded of the story of the mountain that was reduced to a plain because a single grain was stolen from it each day for centuries."

Ooka nodded gravely. "It is just as dishonest to steal one grain of rice as it is to steal a large sack," he remarked. "Did you take proper steps to guard your property?"

"Yes, my lord. I stationed a guard with the rice each night, but still it disappears. I cannot understand it," the rice merchant said, pulling his white beard nervously.

"What about your guard. Can he be trusted?" Ooka asked.

"Absolutely, Lord Ooka," Yahichi said. "The guard is Chogoro. He has served my family for seventy-five years."

"Yes, I know Chogoro," Ooka said. "He is a most conscientious man. He could not be the thief. But it is possible that he falls asleep at his post. After all, he is eighty years old."

"A man can be just as alert at eighty as at twenty," Yahichi replied quickly. "I am eighty-one myself, and I have never been so alert. Besides, I stood guard myself with Chogoro these last two nights. The rice vanished just the same."

"In that case I will watch with you tonight," Ooka said. "I should like to see this for myself."

As he had promised, Ooka made his way that evening to Yahichi's rice store. He was sure that both Yahichi and Chogoro had fallen asleep and had allowed the thief to enter each time the rice had been stolen, and it was not long before his suspicions were proved correct. Within an hour, both men were sleeping soundly. Ooka smiled. He was certain that when the men awoke neither would admit he had slept at all.

A little past midnight, Ooka heard a slight sound outside the building. He sprang to his feet and peered cautiously out the window. To his astonishment, Ooka found himself staring straight into the face of a man standing in the shadows just outside the building. The judge recognized him as Gonta, a laborer who had been out of work for some time. The man was rooted to the spot by fear.

Ooka hesitated to arrest him. After all, he had not entered the rice store. Ooka would have no proof that he had come to steal. He could simply say that he had lost his way in the dark.

Though Ooka had recognized the thief, Gonta had not recognized the judge, for the darkness inside the building hid his face.

Ooka decided the best thing to do would be to pretend that he, too, was a thief. In this way he might trap Gonta into completing his crime. Speaking in a harsh tone to disguise his voice, he said, "You have obviously come here to steal rice just as I have."

Gonta was relieved to find himself face to face with another thief instead of a guard.

"As a favor from one thief to another," Ooka continued, "I will pass the rice out to you, so that you will not need to risk coming in yourself."

Gonta thanked him profusely for his courtesy, and Ooka picked up a large sack of rice and handed it out to him.

"This is too much," Gonta protested. "I want only a few handfuls."

Ooka was amazed. "But if you are going to steal, you may as well take a large amount. After all, if Ooka catches you, you will be punished as much for stealing a single grain as you would for a whole sack."

"That would be dishonest!" Gonta replied indignantly. "I take just enough to feed my family for a single day, for each day I hope

I will find work and not have to steal anymore. If I do find work, I intend to return all I have taken."

Then he took out the amount of rice he needed for his family's daily meal and handed the sack back to the astonished judge. Thanking Ooka once more for his courtesy, Gonta turned and disappeared into the darkness. Ooka did not try to stop him.

When the shopkeeper and his guard awoke, Ooka told them what had happened.

"But why did you let the thief go?" Yahichi asked indignantly.

"Gonta is certainly a thief," Ooka replied. "But I am convinced he is an honest one, for he refused to steal more than he needed."

"But, Lord Ooka, how can a man be a thief and honest at the same time?"

"I would never have believed it possible, but it is so," Ooka said. "It is the duty of a judge to punish wickedness and reward virtue. In this case, we find both qualities in the same man, so obviously it would be unfair to treat him as any ordinary thief."

"But, Lord Ooka—"

"I have made my decision. Tomorrow I will see that work is found for Gonta which is sufficient to feed his family and still leave enough to allow him to pay back the rice he stole. We will see if he keeps his promise. If he returns here and replaces the extra amount each night, it will prove my belief that he is an honest thief."

The plan was carried out according to Ooka's wishes. Gonta was given a job, without knowing that Ooka was responsible. And, as the judge suspected, every night Gonta took the rice left over from his day's earnings and left it in the rice shop.

Ooka put all kinds of obstacles in his way to make it difficult for him to enter the shop, but this did not prevent Gonta from returning each night, although he became more and more afraid of being caught.

Yahichi admitted that the thief had been punished enough for his crime and told Ooka he did not wish to press charges. The great judge smiled and wrote out a small scroll which he ordered Yahichi to leave for Gonta to see when he came to pay for the last portion of rice.

When the honest thief slipped fearfully into the rice shop for the last time, he was shocked to find the scroll on which was written in Ooka's own handwriting, and bearing Ooka's signature, the following message:

You owe an extra ten percent for interest. Honesty is the best policy.

Papa and I rowed out on the Quabbin Reservoir.

Letting Swift River Go

Jane Yolen

AUTHOR'S NOTE

The Quabbin Reservoir is near my house,
one of the largest bodies of fresh water in
   New England.
It is a lovely wilderness;
eagles soar overhead and deer mark out
   their paths.
But once it was a low-lying valley called
   Swift River,
surrounded by rugged hills.
There were towns in the valley filled with
   hardworking folks
whose parents and grandparents had lived
   there all their lives.

Then, between 1927 and 1946, all the houses
and churches and schools—the markers of
   their lives—
were gone forever under the rising waters.

The drowning of the Swift River towns
to create the Quabbin was not a unique event.
The same story—only with different names—
has occurred all over the world
wherever nearby large cities have had
   powerful thirsts.
Such reservoirs are trade-offs, which,
   like all trades,
are never easy, never perfectly fair.

When I was six years old
the world seemed a very safe place.
The wind whispered comfortably
through the long branches
of the willow by my bedroom window.
Mama let me walk to school all alone
along the winding blacktop,
past the Old Stone Mill,
past the Grange Hall,
past our church,
not even meeting up with
Georgie Warren or Nancy Vaughan
till the crossroads.

Georgie and I fished the Swift River
in the bright days of summer,
catching brown trout out of the pools
with a pin hook and a bit of thread.
We played mumblety-peg
in the graveyard
and picnicked on Grandpa Will's stone,
the black one that stayed warm all day
by soaking up the hot summer sun.

And many a summer night
I slept out under the backyard maples
with Nancy Vaughan.
We'd listen to the trains
starting and stopping along Rabbit Run,
their long whistles lowing into the dark,
startling the screech owl
off its perch on the great elm.
Lying there, looking up
at the lengthening shadows of trees,
we'd see the fireflies
winking on and off and on.

• JANE YOLEN •

One night Nancy Vaughan
and her cousin Sara from the city
brought three mason jars to my house.
We caught fireflies in them,
holding our hands over the open tops.
Mama came out to watch.
She shook her head.
"You have to let them go, Sally Jane,"
she said to me.
So I did.

In the deep winter
Papa harvested ice
from Greenwich Lake,
and Mama kept the stove going
in the house all day and all night.
I slept under three eiderdowns
and Grandma's quilt.
Later, in March,
we put buckets up on all the maples,
dipping our fingers down into the sap
and tasting the thin sweetness.

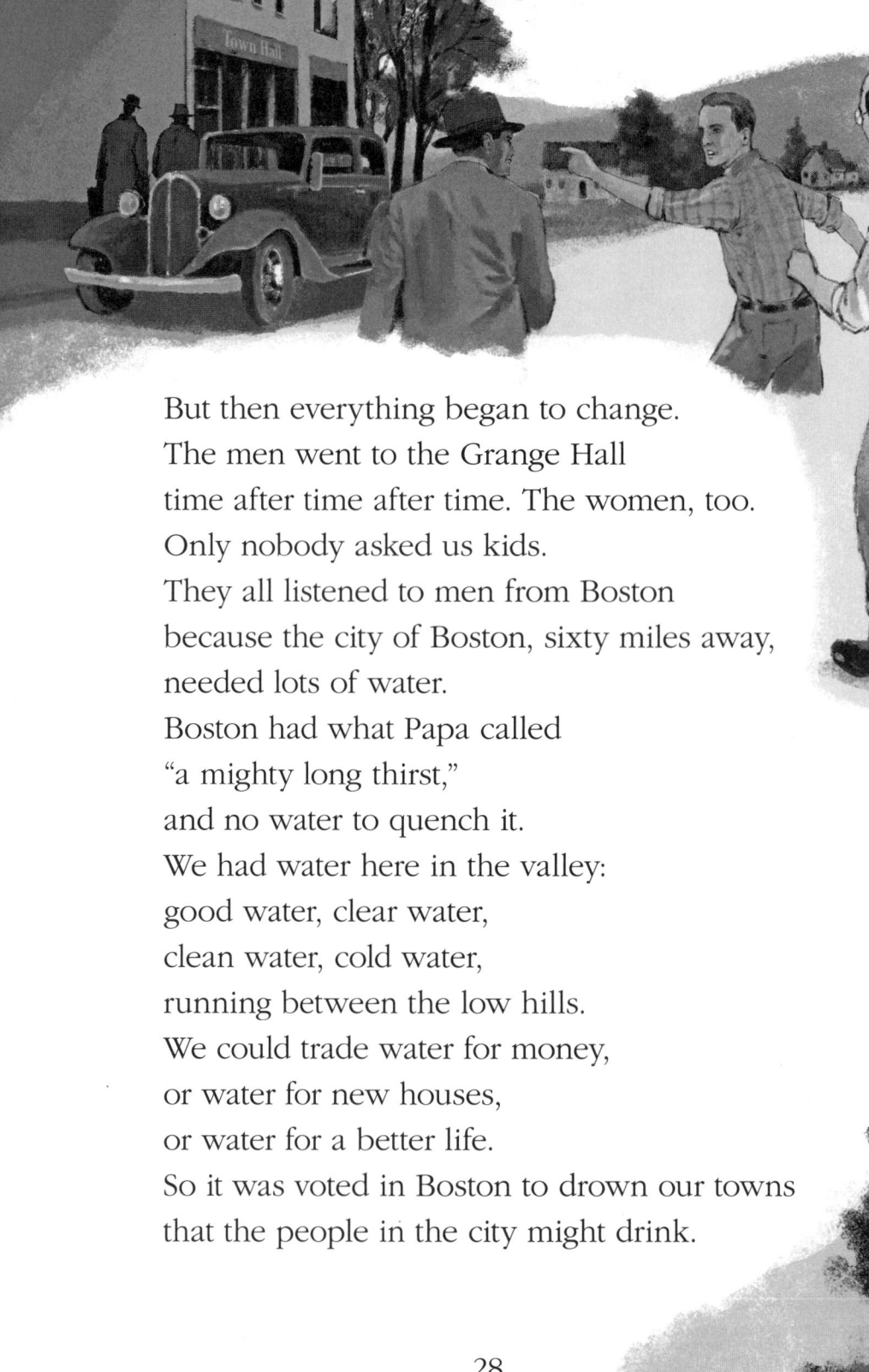

But then everything began to change.
The men went to the Grange Hall
time after time after time. The women, too.
Only nobody asked us kids.
They all listened to men from Boston
because the city of Boston, sixty miles away,
needed lots of water.
Boston had what Papa called
"a mighty long thirst,"
and no water to quench it.
We had water here in the valley:
good water, clear water,
clean water, cold water,
running between the low hills.
We could trade water for money,
or water for new houses,
or water for a better life.
So it was voted in Boston to drown our towns
that the people in the city might drink.

First we moved the graves:
Grandpa Will's black stone,
and the Doubledays and the Downings,
the Metcalfs and the Halls.
Papa read the headstones on the trucks
as he helped gather the small remains,
hauling them to the new cemetery
where everything would be fresh and green.
Sometimes all the men
found were buttons or teeth
or a few thin bones.
Papa said they left the Indians
where they lay.
No one wanted to bother with them,
but I thought it right
they remain in sacred ground.
The blackflies were fierce,
Papa said, fierce.
He had bites under his eyes,
swollen like tears.

Then the governor sent his "woodpeckers"
to clear the scrub and brush,
to cut down all the trees:
the maples and elms,
the willows and sycamores,
and the great spreading oaks.
They were stacked like drinking straws
along the roads,
then hauled away.

Our houses came next.
Some were bulldozed.
One great push and they went over
after one and two centuries
of standing strong
against wind and snow and rain.
Georgie and I watched them push down
the Old Stone Mill
till the windows of one wall
stared out like empty eyes
at the far-off hills.

• JANE YOLEN •

Mr. Baxter's house went by truck
along the blacktop
to its new home in another town,
slow as any child going to school.
Nancy and I ran alongside for a ways,
but it had more breath than we did.
We stopped, panting,
and watched till it was out of sight.
Then Mama and Papa and I
moved away to New Salem,
one big hill over, and into a tiny house
where my room was warm all winter long.
Nancy and her folks went to the city
to be near her cousin Sara.
I never heard where Georgie went,
never even got to say good-bye.

Strangers came with their big machines,
building tunnels and caissons,
the Winsor Dam and the Goodnough Dike.
Papa brought me over to watch
most Friday afternoons.
"You've got to remember, Sally Jane," he said.
"Remember our town."
But it didn't *seem* like our town anymore.
There were no trees, no bushes,
no gardens, no fences,
no houses, no churches, no barns, no halls.
Just a long, gray wilderness,
just a hole between hills.

The water from the dammed rivers
moved in slowly and silently.
They rose like unfriendly neighbors
halfway up the sides of the hills,
covering Dana and Enfield,
Prescott and Greenwich,
all the little Swift River towns.
It took seven long years.

Much later, when I was grown,
Papa and I rowed out on the Quabbin Reservoir.
Behind us we left a bubble trail.
Through the late afternoon
and well into the evening
we sat in the little boat
and Papa pointed over the side.
"Look, Sally Jane," he said,
"that's where the road to Prescott ran,
there's the road to Beaver Brook,
that's the spot the church stood
where we had you baptized.
And the school.
And the Grange Hall.
And the Old Stone Mill.
We won't be seeing those again."
I looked.
I thought I could see the faint outlines,
but I could not read the past.
Little perch now owned those streets,
and bass swam over the country roads.
A rainbow trout leaped after a fly,
and the water rings rippled through
my father's careful mapping.

When it got dark
the stars came out,
reflecting in the water,
winking on and off and on like fireflies.
I leaned over the side of the boat
and caught the starry water
in my cupped hands.
For a moment I remembered
the wind through the willow,
the trains whistling on Rabbit Run,
the crossroads where I had met
Georgie Warren and Nancy Vaughan.
Gone, all gone, under the waters.

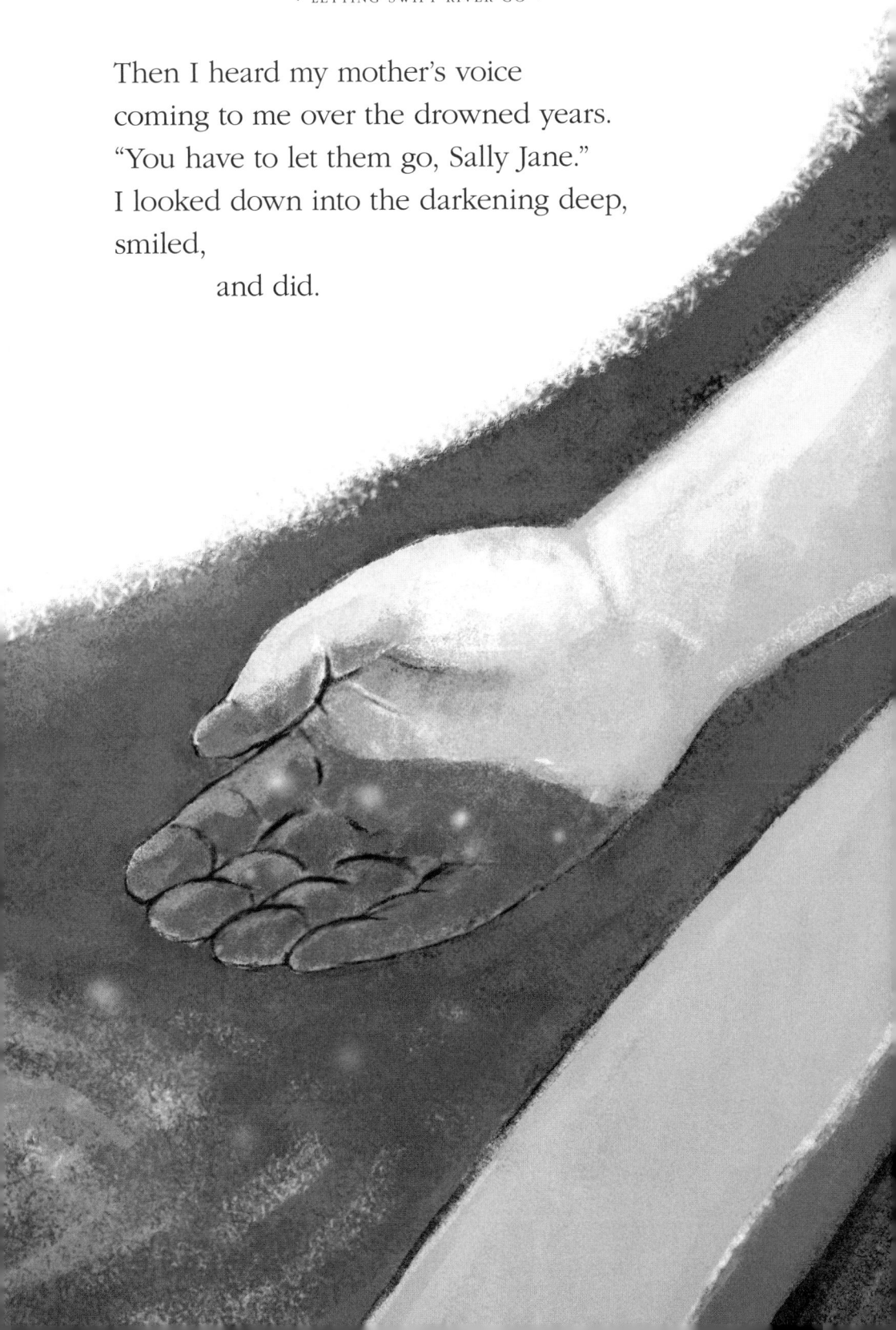

Then I heard my mother's voice
coming to me over the drowned years.
"You have to let them go, Sally Jane."
I looked down into the darkening deep,
smiled,
      and did.

"The Emperor is in his dressing room right now."

The Emperor's New Clothes

Hans Christian Andersen

Many years ago there lived an Emperor who cared so much about beautiful new clothes that he spent all his money on dressing stylishly. He took no interest at all in his soldiers, nor did he care to attend the theater or go out for a drive, unless of course it gave him a chance to show off his new clothes. He had a different outfit for every hour of the day and, just as you usually say that kings are sitting in council, it was always said of him: "The Emperor is in his dressing room right now."

In the big city where the Emperor lived, there were many distractions. Strangers came and went all the time, and one day two swindlers appeared. They claimed to be weavers and said that they knew how to weave the loveliest cloth you could imagine. Not only were the colors and designs they created unusually beautiful, but the clothes made from their fabrics also had the amazing ability of becoming invisible to those who were unfit for their posts or just hopelessly stupid.

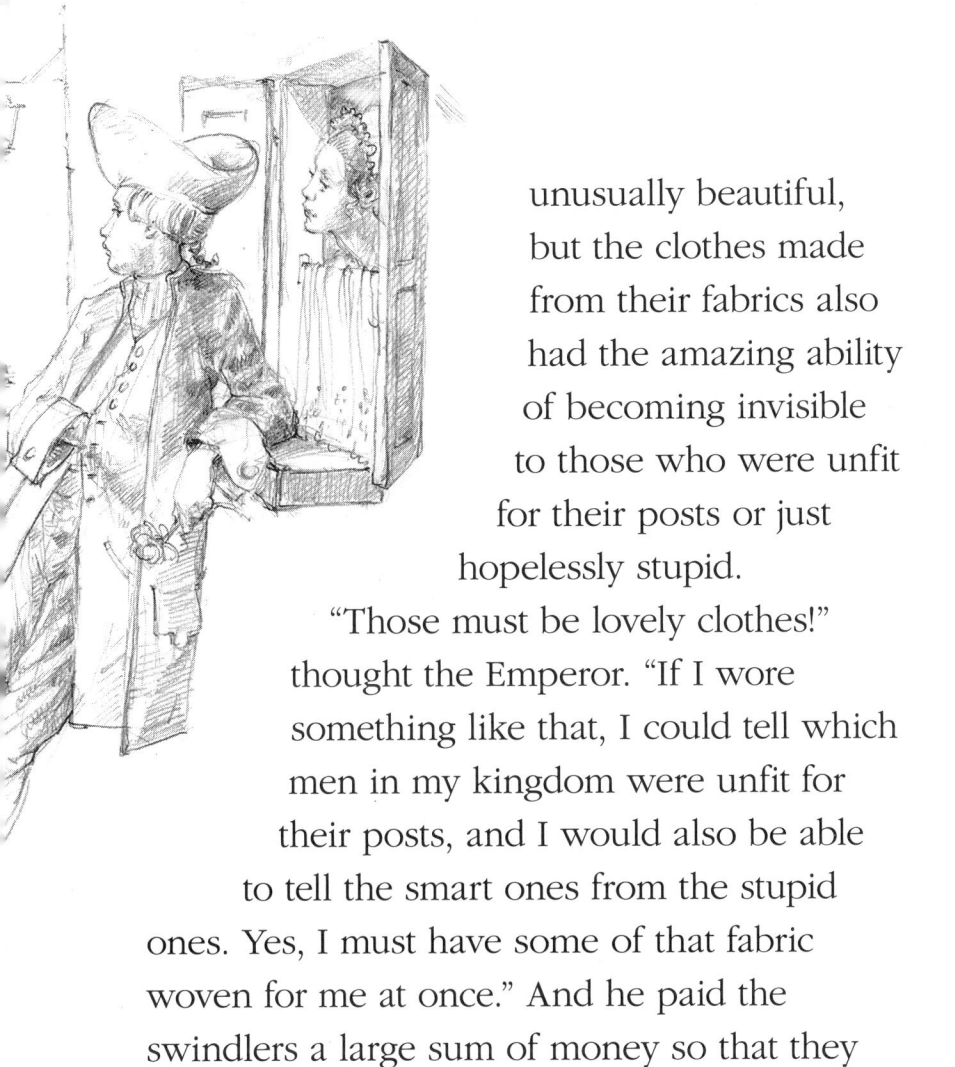

"Those must be lovely clothes!" thought the Emperor. "If I wore something like that, I could tell which men in my kingdom were unfit for their posts, and I would also be able to tell the smart ones from the stupid ones. Yes, I must have some of that fabric woven for me at once." And he paid the swindlers a large sum of money so that they could get started at once.

The swindlers assembled a couple of looms and pretended to be working, but there was nothing at all on their looms. Straightaway they demanded the finest silk and the purest gold thread, which they promptly stowed away in their own bags. Then they worked far into the night on their empty looms.

"Well, now, I wonder how the weavers are getting on with their work," the Emperor thought. But he was beginning to feel some anxiety about the fact that anyone who was stupid or unfit for his post would not be able to see what was being woven. Not that he had any fears about himself—he felt quite confident on that score—but all the same it might be better to send someone else out first, to see how things were progressing. Everyone in town had heard about the cloth's mysterious power, and they were all eager to discover the incompetence or stupidity of their neighbors.

"I will send my honest old minister to the weavers," the Emperor thought. "He's the best person to inspect the cloth, for he has plenty of good sense, and no one is better qualified for his post than he is."

So off went the good-natured old minister to the workshop where the two swindlers were laboring with all their might at the empty looms. "God save us!" thought the minister, and his eyes nearly popped out of his head. "Why, I can't see a thing!" But he was careful not to say that out loud.

The two swindlers invited him to take a closer look—didn't he find the pattern beautiful and the colors lovely? They gestured at the empty frames, but no matter how widely he opened his eyes, he couldn't see a thing, for there was nothing there. "Good Lord!" he thought. "Is it possible that I'm an idiot? I never once suspected it, and I mustn't let on that it is a possibility. Can it be that I'm unfit for my post? No, it will never do for me to admit that I can't see the cloth."

"Well, why aren't you saying anything about it?" asked one of the swindlers, who was pretending to be weaving.

"Oh, it's enchanting! Quite exquisite!" the old minister said, peering over his spectacles. "That pattern and those colors! I shall tell the Emperor right away how much I like it."

"Ah, we are so glad that you like it," the weavers replied, and they described the colors and extraordinary patterns in detail. The old minister listened attentively so that he would be able to repeat their description to the Emperor when he returned home—which he duly did.

The swindlers demanded more money, more silk, and more gold thread, which they insisted they needed to keep weaving. They stuffed it all in their own pockets—not a thread was put on the loom—while they went on weaving at the empty frames as before.

After a while, the Emperor sent a second respected official to see how the weaving was progressing and to find out when the cloth would be ready. What had happened to the first minister also happened to him. He looked as hard as he could, but since there was nothing there but an empty loom, he couldn't see a thing.

"There, isn't this a beautiful piece of cloth!" the swindlers declared, as they described the lovely design that didn't exist at all.

"I'm not stupid," thought the man. "This can only mean that I'm not fit for my position. That would be ridiculous, so I'd better not let on." And so he praised the cloth he could not see and declared that he was delighted with its beautiful hues and lovely patterns. "Yes, it's quite exquisite," he said to the Emperor.

The splendid fabric soon became the talk of the town.

And now the Emperor wanted to see the cloth for himself while it was still on the loom. Accompanied by a select group of people, including the two stately old officials who had already been there, he went to visit the crafty swindlers, who were weaving for all they were worth without using a bit of yarn or thread.

"Look, isn't it *magnifique*?" the two venerable officials exclaimed. "If Your Majesty will but take a look. What a design! What colors!" And they pointed at the empty loom, feeling sure that all the others could see the cloth.

"What on earth!" thought the Emperor. "I can't see a thing! This is appalling! Am I stupid? Am I unfit to be Emperor? This is the most horrible thing I can imagine happening to me!"

"Oh, it's very beautiful!" the Emperor said. "It has our most gracious approval." And he gave a satisfied nod as he inspected the empty loom. He wasn't about to say that he couldn't see a thing. The courtiers who had come with him strained their eyes, but they couldn't see any more than the others. Still, they all said exactly what the Emperor had said: "Oh, it's very beautiful!" They advised him to wear his splendid new clothes for the first time in the grand parade that was about to take place.

"It's *magnifique*!" "Exquisite!" "Superb!"—that's what you heard over and over again. Everyone was really pleased with the weaving. The Emperor knighted each of the two swindlers and gave them medals to wear in their buttonholes, along with the title Imperial Weaver.

On the eve of the parade, the rogues sat up all night with more than sixteen candles burning. Everyone could see how busy they were finishing the Emperor's new clothes. They pretended to remove the cloth from the loom; they cut the air with big scissors; and they sewed with needles that had no thread. Then at last they announced: "There! The Emperor's clothes are ready at last!"

The Emperor, with his most distinguished courtiers, went in person to the weavers, who each stretched out an arm as if holding something up and said: "Just look at these trousers! Here is the jacket! This is the cloak." And so on. "They are all as light as spiderwebs. You can hardly tell you are wearing anything— that's the virtue of this delicate cloth."

"Yes, indeed," the courtiers declared. But they were unable to see a thing, for there was absolutely nothing there.

"Now, would it please His Imperial Majesty to remove his clothes?" asked the swindlers. "Then we can fit you with the new ones, over there in front of the long mirror."

And so the Emperor took off the clothes he was wearing, and the swindlers pretended to hand him each of the new garments they claimed to have made, and they held him at the waist as if they were attaching something . . . it was his train. And the Emperor twisted and turned in front of the mirror.

"Goodness! How splendid His Majesty looks in the new clothes. What a perfect fit!" they all exclaimed. "What patterns! What colors! What priceless attire!"

The master of ceremonies came in with an announcement. "The canopy for the parade is ready and waiting for Your Majesty."

"I am quite ready," said the Emperor. "The clothes suit me well, don't they!" And he turned around one last time in front of the mirror, trying to look as if he were examining his fine new clothing.

The chamberlains who were supposed to carry the train groped around on the floor as if they were picking it up. As they walked, they held out their hands, not daring to let on that they couldn't see anything.

The Emperor marched in the parade under the lovely canopy, and everyone in the streets and at the windows said: "Goodness! The Emperor's new clothes are the finest he has ever worn. What a lovely train on his coat! What a perfect fit!" People were not willing to let on that there was nothing at all to see, because that would have meant they were either unfit for their posts or very stupid. Never had the Emperor's clothes made such a great impression.

"But he isn't wearing anything at all!" a little child declared.

"Goodness gracious! Did you hear the voice of that innocent child!" cried the father. And the child's remark was whispered from one person to the next.

"Yes, he isn't wearing anything at all!" the crowd shouted at last. And the Emperor cringed, for he was beginning to suspect that everyone was right. But then he realized: "I must go through with it now, parade and all." And he drew himself up even more proudly than before, while his chamberlains walked behind him carrying the train that was not there at all.

Glossary

In this glossary, you will find the meanings of words that are in the Junior Great Books stories you have read. If a word that you are wondering about is not listed here, go to your dictionary for help.

Aa

admit: When you **admit** something, you tell the truth about it. *The thief had to **admit** he stole the wallet when it was discovered in his bag.*

anxiety: When you have **anxiety**, you are very worried or nervous about what might happen. *You might be filled with **anxiety** the night before a test if you knew you were not ready for it.*

appalling: Terrible or shocking. *You might not be allowed to see some movies because your parents think the violence in them is **appalling**.*

approval: To give your **approval** to something means that you officially agree with it or that you have a good opinion of it. *You might need your parents' **approval** before you go to a sleepover at a friend's house. The dog won first place at the dog show because it had the **approval** of all the judges.*

astonishment: When you feel **astonishment**, you feel so surprised that you can't believe it. *You might feel **astonishment** if you were given ice cream for breakfast.*

attire: Clothing.

Cc

chamberlains: The people in charge of the household of a royal person.

charges: A **charge** is an official statement saying that someone has done something illegal or wrong. When you **press charges**, you officially blame a person for committing a crime. *My neighbor wants to **press charges** against the man who broke her window and take him to court.*

conscientious: If you are **conscientious**, you know right from wrong, and you do what you think is right. *A **conscientious** student would not cheat on a test.* Being **conscientious** also means taking the time to do things carefully and completely. *I was **conscientious** and double-checked my homework for spelling mistakes.*

council: A group of people brought together to help solve problems, give advice, or make laws. *The king asked his **council** of wise men and women to help him decide the laws of the kingdom.*

courtesy: Politeness and thoughtfulness; showing good manners. *You show **courtesy** when you write thank-you notes for your birthday presents.*

courtiers: People who spend time with and help a royal person. ***Courtiers** might wait on a king or queen, helping them dress or bringing them meals.*

cringed: To **cringe** is to pull your head or body away from something because of a feeling of fear, embarrassment, or dislike. *You might **cringe** if someone was pointing and laughing at you. The puppy **cringed** when it heard the thunder and lightning outside.*

Dd

demanded: To **demand** is to order something to be done or to ask for something firmly. *The ice cream seller **demanded** payment before making my cone.*

distinguished: People who are **distinguished** are respected or famous because of their talents or skills. *The **distinguished** author has won many awards for her wonderful books.*

duly: To do something **duly** means to do it at the proper time or in the correct way. *When the teacher told us it was time for reading, we **duly** took out our books. My father **duly** paid the check after we finished our dinner at the restaurant.*

Ee

exquisite: Something **exquisite** is very beautiful or very finely made. *The pink and orange sunset over the ocean is **exquisite**. The **exquisite** pattern on her coat was stitched by hand.*

Ff

fierce: Nasty, strong, or violent. *You should never get close to very **fierce** animals or they may bite, scratch, or kick you. The **fierce** wind knocked over a tree in our front yard.*

Gg

gestured: To **gesture** is to make movements with your body or head to show what you are thinking or feeling. *The crossing guard **gestured** for us to stop by holding out her hand.*

gravely: When you do or say something **gravely**, you do it in a very serious way. *The news reporter spoke **gravely** about the car accident. The man looked **gravely** at the children who broke his window.*

groped: To **grope** is to feel around with your hands for something you cannot see. *I **groped** for the light switch in the dark room.*

Hh

harvested: To **harvest** is to gather crops when they are ready. *We **harvested** our berries quickly because there were many people picking them.*

hauling: Hauling is pulling something with force to move it. ***Hauling** can often be done by truck or by cart. The men are **hauling** the heavy tree branches away by tying ropes to them and pulling them along.*

hesitate: To **hesitate** is to wait before you do something because you do not feel sure about it. *A baby who is just learning to walk might **hesitate** before he takes a step.*

hues: Colors. *A peacock's tail has many **hues**, including blue, green, and purple.*

Ii

impression: An **impression** is a feeling, an idea, or an opinion about someone or something. *He tried to make a good **impression** at school by working hard and being polite to his teachers. I have an **impression** that she doesn't like me because she never invites me to any of her parties.*

indignantly: If you do or say something **indignantly**, you are upset and angry because you feel that something is not fair. *She stomped off to her room **indignantly** when her parents punished her for something she didn't do.*

inspect: To **inspect** something is to look very closely at it. *I had to **inspect** the sleeve of my sweater to find the tiny hole in it.*

interest: An extra amount of money that must be paid when someone borrows money. *If the bank lends her money to buy a house, she will need to pay the bank back all the money plus some **interest**.*

Ll

lengthening: Growing longer.

let on: To **let on** means to show or admit that you know something. *My best friend **let on** that she was planning a birthday party for me and spoiled the surprise.*

looms: Looms are frames or machines used to weave thread or yarn into cloth.

Pp

panting: **Panting** is fast and hard breathing. *The runners were **panting** after they finished the long race.*

posts: Jobs.

profusely: When you do something **profusely**, you do it many times—maybe even more than enough. *I apologized **profusely** for hitting my friend with the ball while we were playing catch.*

promptly: When something is done **promptly**, it is done quickly or right away. *We went **promptly** to the theater when we found out the movie was starting in fifteen minutes.*

Qq

qualified: If you are **qualified** for something, you have the skills or the knowledge to do it. *Once I take some first aid classes, I will be **qualified** to be a lifeguard at the pool.*

quench: To **quench** something is to put an end to it or to satisfy it. *You might **quench** your thirst with a large glass of water.*

Rr

reflecting: When something is **reflecting**, it is showing back a picture of something on a shiny surface, like a mirror. *The window glass is **reflecting** my face.*

ridiculous: Very silly or foolish. *She wore a **ridiculous** hat with plastic fruit and flowers all over it.*

rogues: A **rogue** is a person who plays tricks or misbehaves. *A **rogue** stole my lunch money yesterday. Those two **rogues** are always throwing snowballs at the school bus!*

Ss

scroll: A roll of paper or parchment (specially prepared animal skin) with writing on it. *Each end of a **scroll** is usually wrapped around a rod.*

scrub: Short, skinny bushes or trees. ***Scrub** is not very strong or tall and it is easier to pull out than fully grown trees or bushes.*

startling: Startling someone or something means scaring or surprising them into making a sudden movement. *The noise of the fireworks keeps **startling** the birds that live in the park. My sister sneaked up behind me and tapped my shoulder, **startling** me out of my chair.*

stately: A **stately** person looks and acts in a noble way. *The king walked in a **stately** manner with his chest out and his head held high.*

sufficient: Enough, or as much as someone would need or want. *I'm not very hungry, so half a sandwich will be **sufficient** for lunch.*

suspicions: When you have **suspicions**, you are pretty sure something is wrong or bad, but you don't know for certain. *I had **suspicions** that the man had stolen something when I saw him run quickly out of the store.*

swindlers: Swindlers are people who take other people's money or property by tricking them. *The **swindlers** pretended to raise the money for charity, but they kept it for themselves instead.*

Tt

train: A long part of a robe or dress that trails behind the person wearing it.

Vv

venerable: Someone **venerable** is worthy of respect because of his or her age, knowledge, or position in life. *The children asked their **venerable** grandmother to sit at the head of the table.*

virtue / wilderness

virtue: When you behave with **virtue**, it means you know and do what is right. *When you are honest, kind, or helpful, you are showing **virtue**.*

Ww

wilderness: A wild natural area where no people live. *A **wilderness** might have lots of trees and plants, like a forest or a jungle, or it might be bare, like a desert.*

ACKNOWLEDGMENTS

All possible care has been taken to trace ownership and secure permission for each selection in this series. The Great Books Foundation wishes to thank the following authors, publishers, and representatives for permission to reprint copyrighted materials:

Ooka and the Honest Thief, from OOKA THE WISE: TALES OF OLD JAPAN, by I. G. Edmonds. Copyright © 1961, 1994 by I. G. Edmonds. Reprinted by permission of Barry N. Malzberg.

LETTING SWIFT RIVER GO, by Jane Yolen. Copyright © 1987 by Jane Yolen. Reprinted by permission of Little, Brown and Company.

The Emperor's New Clothes, by Hans Christian Andersen, from THE ANNOTATED HANS CHRISTIAN ANDERSEN, edited by Maria Tatar. Translated by Maria Tatar and Julie K. Allen. Copyright © 2008 by Maria Tatar. Reprinted by permission of W. W. Norton and Company, Inc.

ILLUSTRATION CREDITS

Leo and Diane Dillon prepared the illustrations for *Ooka and the Honest Thief.*

Rich Lo prepared the illustrations for *Letting Swift River Go.*

Brock Cole prepared the illustrations for *The Emperor's New Clothes.*

Cover art by Rich Lo.

Design by THINK Book Works.